Cambridge English Readers

Level 2

Series editor

Within High Fences

Penny Hancock

CAMBRIDGE
UNIVERSITY PRESS

CAMBRIDGE
UNIVERSITY PRESS

University Printing House, Cambridge CB2 8BS, United Kingdom

Cambridge University Press is part of the University of Cambridge.

It furthers the University's mission by disseminating knowledge in the pursuit of education, learning and research at the highest international levels of excellence.

www.cambridge.org
Information on this title: www.cambridge.org/9780521605601

© Cambridge University Press 2005

This publication is in copyright. Subject to statutory exception and to the provisions of relevant collective licensing agreements, no reproduction of any part may take place without the written permission of Cambridge University Press.

First published 2005
Reprinted 2016

Printed in the United Kingdom by Hobbs the Printers Ltd

A catalogue record for this publication is available from the British Library

ISBN 978-0-521-60560-1 Paperback

Cambridge University Press has no responsibility for the persistence or accuracy of URLs for external or third-party internet websites referred to in this publication, and does not guarantee that any content on such websites is, or will remain, accurate or appropriate. Information regarding prices, travel timetables and other factual information given in this work is correct at the time of first printing but Cambridge University Press does not guarantee the accuracy of such information thereafter.

Contents

People in the story

Nancy: a guard
Tom: Nancy's boyfriend
George: an asylum seeker
Harriet: Nancy's best friend
Steve: Harriet's boyfriend
Bill: works with Nancy

Chapter 1 *Night work*

There was nothing different about that night. It was the same as every other night, I thought. But that night, my life started to change. I didn't know it then, but I know it now.

It was a January evening and it was cold and dark. I was leaving to go to work and I was wearing my uniform. Tom, my boyfriend, was watching a DVD.

'Bye, Tom,' I said.

He didn't answer.

'Tom?'

'You know I don't like you working at night,' he said. He said this every night. He kissed me, but the kiss felt cold.

I walked out of the front door. We lived in a comfortable new house in Greenwich, South East London. I thought I knew who I was. I thought I knew what I wanted. I had Tom . . . my man. He was older than me, tall with blond hair and blue eyes. He liked buying me things – clothes, shoes, jewellery – expensive things. For my eighteenth birthday he gave me a gold watch.

We met when I was at school. I wanted to be a writer then. Tom laughed at me. He told me writers were intelligent. 'You're not intelligent,' he said. 'You're beautiful, but you're not intelligent.' And I believed him.

I moved in with him when I finished school. I didn't think about the rest of my life. I thought I was in love. Tom was all I wanted.

That night I started the car and drove through the dark. It was very cold. As I drove I thought about Tom. I put my hand up to my face. I could feel his cold kiss on my cheek.

Tom said the night was his time with me. He said I didn't need to work. It wasn't a great job but I liked the money. And I liked shopping. Now I could buy the things *I* wanted. For the first time in my life, I was earning some money. For the first time in my life, I didn't need Tom for everything.

Chapter 2   *Within high fences*

I arrived at work. I showed my identity card to the guards and drove through the gates.

I stopped my car, got out and walked to the next gates. I showed my identity card again to some more guards. Then they opened the gates and let me in.

I was now at work. I worked in a centre for asylum seekers – people who want to live in Great Britain because of bad problems in their countries.

When I first started working as a guard, I didn't know much about asylum seekers. Now, I was beginning to understand more about the people I was guarding.

Sometimes asylum seekers come to this country because there is terrible fighting in their countries and they are afraid. Asylum seekers come here because they hope they will have a better life in Britain.

When they arrive, asylum seekers wait to know who can stay, and who must go home to their countries. Sometimes the asylum seekers wait in the centre for days, sometimes for weeks and sometimes for months.

We were all locked in together. At the end of every night's work, I could go home, but the asylum seekers had to stay in the centre.

When you have a lot of people together in one place, you have to have rules. Rules tell people what they can and can't do. I didn't always agree with the rules. But I had to make sure everybody followed them. It was my job.

I went to the dining room. Dinner was finished, but there was nowhere else to go. Most of the asylum seekers spent their time here. But there was nothing to do. The tables and chairs and walls were grey. I walked around the dining room and looked at all the faces. Some of them were very sad. Some were just tired and afraid. I wanted to make them feel better. I tried to smile. But when they saw my uniform, they looked away. To them, my uniform said 'I am not your friend'.

People were waiting for a cup of tea or coffee, and a

biscuit. Bill, one of the other guards, was watching them.

I saw a woman at a table. She had a little boy with her. They both looked really sad, really tired.

'Do you want some tea or coffee?' I asked the woman.

She didn't understand.

I began to speak again, but there was a shout. The woman and the child looked up. They looked really afraid. Bill was shouting at a tall man.

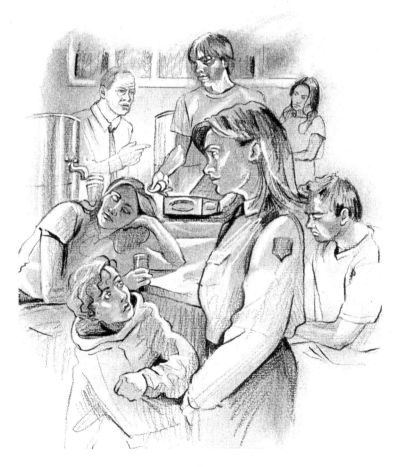

'Put it back!' he shouted. 'I saw you. You were stealing!'

The tall man had black hair and dark eyes. He looked down at Bill.

'Steal?' he said.

'Yes,' said Bill. 'You took something that wasn't yours!'

The tall man looked at the two biscuits in his hand.

'But this is a *biscuit*!' said the man angrily. 'It isn't something expensive!'

'You can only have *one* biscuit. It's the rules. You took two,' said Bill.

'But this biscuit isn't for me,' said the tall man. 'It's for that boy.' He looked at the little boy with the woman. 'The boy was afraid to take a biscuit. He was afraid of the rules. There are so many rules here.'

'Yes,' said Bill, 'and *you* have to follow the rules.'

The tall man wasn't afraid of Bill's words. He turned and walked away. He gave the two biscuits to the boy and smiled. It was a beautiful smile. The boy was too tired to smile back. He ate the biscuits quickly . . . one, two. He was very hungry. The man smiled at the boy again, and I smiled at the man.

The tall man looked at me for a moment and stopped smiling. Then he turned his back to me.

I wanted to tell him I was a friend. But my uniform said something different. It said 'I am not a friend'. It said 'I agree with all these rules'.

The tall man saw my uniform, and he understood what it said.

But that night, my heart was saying something very different to my uniform.

Chapter 3   *Talking to George*

I finished work at eight o'clock the next morning and drove to the supermarket. I wanted some fruit. I always wanted to eat good things after working in the asylum centre.

At work everything was grey. But outside, there was so much colour. At work, I thought, the only beautiful thing was the tall man's face.

I bought some fruit and drove home. Sometimes, when I got home from work, Tom was still angry with me. But today he wasn't there. He was at work. I was happy to have the house to myself.

I looked at all my things. I looked at the clothes and the shoes in the bedroom; the big expensive television in the living room; my beautiful watch. What did all these things say about me, Nancy Richardson? The asylum seekers didn't have many things. Did I need all these things? I didn't know any more.

I put my favourite music on the CD player. I could see the tall man's face looking at me. He wasn't smiling. Perhaps he didn't like me, I thought. This made me sad. I didn't know why. I didn't know anything about him. But I wanted him to like me.

*   *   *

I was at work, standing near the biscuits and coffee, when I saw the tall man again. He came past and my heart jumped. He put his hand into the box of biscuits.

'Look,' he said. 'Three biscuits. What are you going to do?' His face was hard.

'There are rules here,' I said. 'We all have to follow them.'

'So, what are you going to do?' he said again.

'Nothing,' I said. 'Not all guards shout at people, you know.'

He looked at me. 'That little boy,' he said. 'Hamid. He saw people kill his father and his brother. They tried to kill him, too.'

I couldn't speak.

'He left the country with his mother and they travelled for two weeks to get here. When I gave the boy the biscuits,

I wanted him to feel better. But how could he feel better with just biscuits?'

Most of the time, I didn't think too much about why people left their countries. But this man was making me think and I found it hard.

'Hamid and his mother will get help here,' I said. 'Lawyers will hear their story and help them.'

'I hope so,' he said.

I couldn't stop looking at his face. It was a face that showed so many feelings all at once. It was angry, sad and kind, all at the same time. I wanted to know more about this man.

'And you,' I said quietly. 'Why are you here?'

He didn't speak for a minute. He just looked at me carefully.

Then he said, 'Why are you here yourself?'

I looked away. I was afraid of how I was feeling. 'I'm just doing my job,' I said. I looked back at him. 'My name's Nancy. What's yours?'

'I'm George,' he said. And when he smiled that beautiful smile, my heart jumped again.

'And do you agree with all the rules here?' he asked.

'No,' I replied. 'Not all of them.'

'Then why are you doing this job?'

I didn't know what to say. I did it because I liked having some money.

'I wanted to be a writer,' I replied, 'but I left school early.'

'You can do anything, if you really want to,' said George.

'Maybe,' I said. We talked some more. George was

making me think about things. Writing was something I always loved. Perhaps I could write. Tom was the only person who said I couldn't.

I was changing and there was nothing Tom or I could do about it.

Chapter 4   *The dinner party*

It was Friday night. I wasn't working. Tom and I were going for dinner at my best friend Harriet's house. Harriet and I were old friends from school. We saw each other every week. Harriet lived with her boyfriend, Steve. They were getting married in April, in Scotland.

I put on a red dress and my favourite shoes.

'You look beautiful,' said Tom. He tried to kiss me, but I moved away.

'Come here,' he said and he pulled me hard.

'Stop it, Tom,' I said.

'Why don't you want to kiss me?' he asked.

I didn't reply. I felt angry when Tom was like this.

We didn't talk again as we walked to Harriet and Steve's house.

'Hello. Come in!' said Harriet, opening the door.

I went into the kitchen with Harriet. She was cooking. Harriet is a very good cook. After we left school, she studied to be a cook and I moved in with Tom. In those days, I thought I was the lucky one. I had a man who earned good money and I didn't have to work. Now I wasn't sure. Now I was learning that work can be important.

Harriet knew me better than anyone. She looked at me. 'What's wrong, Nancy?' she asked. 'You look different. What is it?'

I looked at her. 'Don't say I'm stupid,' I said. 'It's about someone at work.'

'At the centre?'

'Yes.'

'A guard?' she asked.

'No,' I said.

'One of the asylum seekers?'

'Yes, I really like him.'

'Like? How?' Harriet asked.

'I think about him all the time.'

'But Nancy, you're with Tom. You and Tom love each other. What more do you want?'

'I don't want more things,' I said. 'The first time I saw this man I . . . I needed him to like me.'

'What's his name?' she asked.

'George.'

'And why did he come to this country?'

'I don't know,' I told her. 'I asked him, but he didn't say.'

'Then what do you know about him?'

I looked at my best friend. 'Harriet,' I said, 'I know that he's kind. I know he wants to help people. Sometimes you don't need to know a lot about someone. I know I like him. That's all.'

Harriet looked at me.

I didn't say anything else. I didn't want to talk about George any more. I didn't think Harriet really understood.

'So, is everything ready for the wedding?' I asked.

'Nancy,' said Harriet, 'just remember, you love Tom. You live with Tom. You have a beautiful home and a good life. Don't lose it.'

Of course Harriet was right. I had a beautiful home. I

had Tom. But I didn't tell Harriet that Tom was often angry with me.

'How's the job?' Steve asked me over dinner.

'It's . . .' I started.

'Why don't they close that centre?' said Tom. 'One day the asylum seekers will all escape. Then we *will* have problems. Asylum seekers steal things.'

I thought about George, Bill and the biscuits.

'Asylum seekers don't steal things, Tom,' I said.

'Well, they come here and take our jobs,' said Tom. 'Soon Nancy will say everyone can come into our country. Then there will be no jobs, no houses and no hospital beds for us!'

'Tom!' said Harriet. 'What are you saying?'

'I'm talking about asylum seekers that come here to get a good life,' said Tom. 'This is *our* country. Not theirs.'

'*Our* country? Who are *we*?' asked Steve.

'Us . . . me . . . people who were born here!'

'So,' said Harriet, 'do you mean that I can't live here because my father was born in Scotland and my mother was born in Italy?' She was as angry as me.

'That's different,' said Tom.

'Why is it different?' asked Harriet.

'I'm talking about people from the other side of the world. They come here and take our jobs and houses.'

'People come to this country because they are afraid to stay in their countries,' I said. 'It isn't easy for them to leave their homes. I hear some terrible stories at the centre. These people need our help.'

Tom laughed.

'Stories! That's what they are. Nancy is so sweet she believes anything. More cake please, Harriet.'

Tom knew we didn't agree with him, so he started talking about something else.

That night, in bed, I couldn't look at Tom.

'The one night I have you at home and you don't want to talk to me!' he said. 'I don't know you any more, Nancy.'

I didn't answer. I waited until he was asleep and then I turned and looked at him. Tom with his angry ideas about asylum seekers. 'Do I still love him?' I asked myself. I closed my eyes but I could see George and not Tom.

Chapter 5   *In danger*

The next time I saw George, he was standing outside the grey building, smoking a cigarette. He smiled at me and my heart jumped.

'Do you want a cigarette?' he asked.

'I don't smoke,' I said. And then I added, 'but I don't mind smoking.'

I looked at him.

'How are you?' I asked.

'I'm OK,' he replied.

'George,' I said, 'why did you come here, to this country?'

I didn't think George wanted to talk about his past. But this time he answered me.

'In my country, I was in danger,' he said.

'Danger? Why?'

'I was a photo journalist,' he said. 'I took some photos for the newspapers, but the police didn't like them. I took them because I wanted people to know what was happening in my country.'

'What were the photos of?' I asked.

'They were of soldiers hurting women and young children. But the police saw my photos and they came to find me.'

'That's terrible,' I said. 'You were trying to help those women and children.'

'Yes,' he said. 'But the police didn't want people to know

what was happening in our country.'

'So what did they do to you?' I asked.

'They locked me in a building and they hurt me. Look.' He opened his shirt and showed me some terrible scars.

'Now you can see why I can't go home.'

I couldn't speak.

'When they let me go, I knew I couldn't work in my country anymore,' George said.

'So you came here?'

'It wasn't easy,' he said. 'But I thought, "when I get to England I can show people my photos. People can see what is really happening in my country." But when I arrived, they brought me to this place. Now I'm locked up again!'

'Only for a short time,' I said. 'They brought you here to keep you safe. A lot of people don't like asylum seekers coming to our country.' I thought of Tom. 'But there are lawyers who can help you. You tell them your story and they will help you.'

'Yes,' he said, 'I hope so. But it's possible they will send me home again. People say it's hard to get asylum here.'

He put out his hand.

'Thank you for listening to me,' he said. 'It helps to talk sometimes.'

I moved away.

'I have to go, George,' I said quickly, and I left.

Something was happening to me. I knew it. I wanted it to happen, but I was afraid.

Really afraid.

Chapter 6 *Against the rules*

I was not allowed to make friends with the asylum seekers. But when George saw me, he always came to talk to me. And I enjoyed talking to George. I tried to stop liking him, but I couldn't.

One evening I was in the dining room helping with the coffee. George was waiting for a drink.

'I talked to some people today,' he said to me as he passed. 'I'm leaving the centre tomorrow.'

My heart jumped.

'Are you staying in this country? Or . . .?' I asked.

'I don't know. They're going to tell me tomorrow.'

I felt afraid for him.

Suddenly I decided to do something – something dangerous. When I started at the centre, they told me never to give anyone my phone number or my address. They told me that I could lose my job. But I didn't want to lose George.

I looked about. Nobody was watching.

'George,' I said. 'Here's my phone number. If you have problems, call me. Perhaps I can help you.' I gave him a piece of paper. 'Thank you,' he said and he put it quickly in his pocket.

He walked away then, without another word.

And the next time I went to work, George was not there.

Chapter 7 *A letter*

After George left, I began to hate my life with Tom.

Every Saturday we went shopping. We bought clothes, CDs and DVDs. Once, I liked shopping. Now when I looked at all the things in the shops, I felt ill.

I thought about George all the time. Where was he? Was he OK? Why didn't he ring me?

Ten days after George left the centre, I arrived at work and there was a letter for me.

I went to a corner of the dining room and opened it.

90 Commercial St
Hackney

Dear Nancy,

I hope you get this. I wanted to write before, but I didn't know what to say.

I can stay here for six months. Maybe longer.

I'm in East London. There are a lot of other asylum seekers here. Some of their stories are very sad.

How are you? How's work? Are you writing any stories?

Please write.

George

I looked at the address at the top of the letter. George was in Hackney! He wasn't very far away from me. For the first time in ten days, I smiled.

Chapter 8 *The meeting*

After I got his letter, I knew that I was falling in love with George. But how could I love him? I lived with Tom. I was a guard. George was an asylum seeker. I knew we couldn't be together. I had to forget about George.

I read his letter many times, but I didn't write back. I wanted to write. But what could I say?

A week later, I was at the supermarket when I got a text message on my phone.

George was here! This time I replied without thinking.

I knew it was wrong to meet George without telling Tom. I knew it was wrong to love him. But I couldn't stop myself.

At three o'clock I was sitting in the bookshop café.

'Nancy.'

I looked up.

'George,' I said.

He looked tired. 'How did you get here?' I asked.

'I came by bus. I wanted to see you again, Nancy.'

He looked at me for a long time.

'You're different without your uniform,' he said.

'Am I?' I didn't know what else to say.

'You look nice,' he said.

I smiled.

'Are you working?' I asked him.

'Not yet. I get a little money but not much. I want to get a camera and take photos. I need to work.'

'I'd like to see your photos,' I said.

'Yes,' he said. 'I think you will understand them. They are photos that show what's really happening to people.'

We talked for a long time. He told me about his life in East London. I told him a little about my life.

Then he said, 'What's the time? I have to be back by half past five.'

I was wearing my gold watch. I looked at it.

'It's half past four.'

'That's a nice watch.'

'Yes,' I said, but I went red.

Did George think I was very rich?

'Did someone buy it for you?'

'It was Tom,' I said quietly.

'Who is Tom?' he asked.

'Tom is the man I live with. But . . .' I stopped. I wanted to tell George that I didn't love Tom anymore. I knew I was falling in love with him. But I didn't know what to say. Then George said it for me.

'Nancy,' he said. 'I feel there is something happening between us.'

'Yes,' I said.

'I need to know, do you give your phone number to all the asylum seekers?'

'No,' I said. 'Just you, George.'

It was then he kissed me.

It was then I knew I was leaving Tom.

Chapter 9   *Walking away*

I left Tom on Monday. When he came home from work, I was waiting by the front door with my bags.

'What are you doing?' Tom asked.

'I'm leaving,' I said quickly.

'What do you mean, leaving?'

'Leaving you.'

'No,' said Tom. 'No, Nancy. You can't. What will you do without me?'

This wasn't easy. I didn't love Tom anymore but I didn't want to hurt him.

'I'm sorry, Tom,' I said. 'Things are different now. I can't stay with you.'

For a few seconds he just looked at me. Then in a very quiet voice, he asked, 'Is there another man?'

I didn't answer him. I felt afraid. Tom was already angry. I didn't want to tell him about George.

'Who is it? Tell me who it is!' Tom was shouting at me.

'I'm not going to tell you,' I said.

'Is it someone you met at that centre?' he asked. 'Is it? Tell me, Nancy.'

'Yes, it is,' I said. 'But I'm not leaving because of him. I'm leaving because I'm learning to think, Tom . . . to think for myself.'

'Who is he?'

'He's called George,' I said. 'And I'm going to help him get asylum, so he can stay in this country.'

Tom stared at me.

'He's an asylum seeker?'

'Yes.'

'And you are going to live with him?'

'No, Tom. I don't know . . . perhaps one day.'

Tom laughed.

'You are stupid, Nancy,' he said. 'I can't believe how stupid you are. This asylum seeker just wants your money and your passport. You hear about people doing this all the time. You'll come back to me, I know you will.'

'No, Tom, never,' I said. 'I'm sorry. But I'm never coming back to live with you.'

Then I took my bags and walked away.

Chapter 10 *Never better*

When I left Tom, I was also leaving a comfortable home, nice things, a car, and Tom's money.

Now I had to find somewhere to live. I didn't earn a lot of money in my job. I had to find somewhere cheap.

I stayed with Harriet for a few days, and she helped me find somewhere to live. It was in a small flat in a house not far away. I was happy to see it was a little nearer to George in Hackney.

A week later I moved in.

Harriet came to see me. 'I brought you some cakes,' she said. She looked around. 'Are you sure you're going to be OK here? It's so small!'

'Yes,' I said. 'It is small. But I don't want a big house anymore. I want to change. I'm going to do something with my life.'

'Don't change too much, Nancy. I like you as you are.'

'Oh, Harriet,' I said. I put my arms around her.

Harriet's wedding was in a few weeks, and I knew she wanted me to be there. But I couldn't go. Not now. It was too difficult.

'Harriet,' I said. 'I'm really sorry . . . but . . . I can't come to your wedding now. People won't talk to me. They won't understand why I left Tom.'

'It's my *wedding*, Nancy,' said Harriet. 'You have to come.'

'Will Tom be there?' I asked.

'I don't know,' said Harriet. 'He's still very angry. He says you're stupid. He says you're with someone who just wants your money and a passport.'

I laughed. 'But I haven't got much money!' I said.

There was a sound at the door.

'This is George now,' I said. 'Please stay Harriet. I want you to meet him.'

I opened the door and George came in.

He looked at me, then at Harriet, then at the cakes on the table.

'Are you Harriet?' he asked.

'Yes,' she said. 'How did you know?'

'Those cakes! Nancy told me about her friend the cook!'

Harriet laughed, and I knew she liked George.

'Please try and come to the wedding,' said Harriet again as she left.

'OK, I'll try,' I said.

'You can bring George.'

I smiled. 'Thank you, Harriet.'

'Bye, Nancy.'

After Harriet left, I went over to George and put my arms around him.

'I'm happy that you met Harriet,' I said. 'She liked you.'

'Nancy,' he replied. 'I'm afraid. Before you met me, you had all these friends. You had money. You had a big house and a garden. Wasn't that a better life for you?'

'No,' I said, 'because you weren't in it.' I pulled George to me and we kissed.

I was changing. I decided to become a writer. I wanted to leave the centre and do something I believed in.

Over the next few weeks George came to see me every day.

The flat was small and I didn't have much money. But I loved George and he loved me. We were happy and life was never better.

Or that's what I thought.

Chapter 11 *Afraid*

It was a Friday evening in April. George and I were standing on the platform at the station. We were waiting for my train to Scotland. I was going to Harriet and Steve's wedding. Harriet told me that Tom was not going. She told me again that she wanted me there. So, I decided to go.

When my train arrived, I kissed George goodbye.

'I love you Nancy,' he said.

'I love you, George,' I told him. I wanted him to come with me, but he didn't want to.

'Your friends won't understand why you're with me and not with Tom,' he said.

'No,' I said, 'you're probably right. It's too soon. But one day they'll understand.'

I put my arms round him and kissed him again.

'I'll see you on Sunday. Use my flat while I'm away. You can stay there.'

My flat was small, but he said it was better than his room.

'I'll be here when your train arrives,' he replied.

*   *   *

The wedding was beautiful, but I thought about George all the time.

As I travelled back to London on the train, I couldn't wait to see George. We were so in love. I knew now that I never really loved Tom. I only thought I loved him. I didn't really know what love was before. And I also knew that George loved me. I couldn't wait to see him – to feel his arms around me.

The train arrived at last. I looked for George. There were a lot of people on the platform. I couldn't see him. I got out of the train and looked around. I waited until the platform was empty, but I still couldn't see him. I felt strange and cold. Was something wrong?

No, I told myself. He had to get a bus here. Buses were often late. But he knew that. Why didn't he leave earlier? Perhaps he was waiting outside. But I didn't see him. I felt afraid. But what was there to be afraid of?

I waited. I waited for a long time. Then I decided to get a taxi home. Perhaps George was ill. The taxi stopped outside my flat. I ran in and I looked about. My drawers and cupboards were open and there were things everywhere.

'George?' I called. No reply. Then I saw that some of my things were not there – my CD player, my small television.

I started looking for my other things. I looked by my bed for the box where I kept my gold watch. I didn't wear it anymore. It made me think of Tom. But I knew it cost a lot of money. It wasn't there! I was afraid. I wanted George.

'George,' I shouted.

But of course, George wasn't there.

Chapter 12 *The police*

I walked slowly around my flat.

'Who got in and took my things?' I thought. 'Only George and Harriet have keys. It couldn't be George. He loves me. But someone came into my flat while I was away.'

I began to feel afraid. I called the police. I didn't want to, but I didn't know what else to do.

A policewoman came to see me.

'Does anyone have a key?' she asked.

'Only my best friend, Harriet, and George. Harriet's away and George is my boyfriend.'

'Have you been with him long?'

'About two months.'

'Where did you meet?' she asked me.

'At work.'

'Does he work with you?' she asked.

'No.'

'So what does he do?'

'He's an asylum seeker. He's waiting for lawyers to tell him he can stay in this country.'

'So he needs papers to work here?' she asked.

'Yes, but he's going to get the papers soon.'

'Is your passport here? Let's go and see please.'

We looked in the cupboard where I kept my passport. It wasn't there.

'Do you have any idea where your boyfriend is?' asked the policewoman. 'We need to talk to him.'

I opened my mouth then closed it again.

I didn't want the police to find George. 'No,' I said. 'I don't know where he is. We saw each other every day before I went to Scotland. But he wasn't here when I got back.'

'OK,' said the policewoman. 'Well, if you see him, please phone us.'

'Of course,' I said. And she left.

The rest of that day I waited. I waited all day for George to call, but he didn't. I tried calling him but there was no answer.

Chapter 13 *Another party*

I couldn't sleep that night.

I lay in bed with my eyes open, thinking and thinking. Did George take my things? Was Tom right? Did George just want my money and my passport?

But then I thought of his beautiful smile. I thought of his kiss. I thought of all the times we talked. George wanted to help people. He wanted to make things better for people. George was not a thief. I knew he wasn't.

At last, I fell asleep at about four o'clock in the morning.

The next few days were terrible. I went to work and, when I got home, I tried to phone George. But he didn't answer.

'Perhaps I could go to his flat,' I thought. His address was at the top of the letter he sent me. 'But perhaps he doesn't want me to find him.'

On Friday evening my phone rang. I answered it quickly. I thought it was George.

'Hi Nancy, it's Harriet. We're back from our holiday. It was wonderful. Paris is so beautiful!

'Good,' I said. 'I'm happy for you.'

'Are you still coming to our party tonight, Nancy?' she asked.

'Oh, I don't know, Harriet.' I forgot she was having a party.

'What's wrong, Nancy? You sound terrible.'

It was good to hear Harriet's kind voice, but I still felt bad. I told her about my flat, and George.

'Oh! Poor, poor Nancy,' she said. 'I can't believe it! That's terrible. But are you sure it was George?'

'No. I don't believe it *was* George! But the police think it was him.'

'You tried phoning him?' she asked.

'Yes. He's not answering.'

'What about his flat? Do you have his address?'

'Yes, but I don't think he wants to see me. He knows where I am. Where is he? Why isn't he here?'

'Nancy, we'll just have to wait and see. I know it's hard for you. But you can't be by yourself after this. You need to be with people. Come to the party, please,' said Harriet.

'I really don't feel like a party,' I replied.

'Oh, come on, Nancy. It'll make you feel better.'

I didn't want to go to a party, but Harriet was right. I didn't want to be by myself.

So that evening, I got the bus to Harriet's house.

She opened the door and put her arms around me.

'Have some champagne,' she said. 'You need something to make you feel better.'

'Thanks, Harriet,' I said.

She gave me a drink in the kitchen. I went into the sitting room. It was full of people.

Everybody was smiling and laughing and talking. I felt more alone than ever.

'Perhaps I'll go home,' I thought, when someone said my name.

Chapter 14 *My old house*

'Nancy!'

My heart stopped for a second.

I looked up. It was Tom. 'Good to see you!' he said. 'How are you?'

'I'm fine,' I answered. I was trying hard to look OK. Inside I felt terrible. I looked at him. Wasn't he still angry with me?

'Have another glass of champagne,' said Tom. 'Tell me about your new life. I want to know!'

'There's not a lot to tell,' I said. 'I've got a new job . . .'

'Here,' he said. He gave me another drink.

He didn't really want to know about my new life.

'Thanks,' I said. The champagne was good after my terrible week. I drank it quickly, then I drank some more.

'You OK?' Tom asked.

'No, Tom. I feel ill. I need to rest but it's so noisy here.'

'Why don't you come back to my house? It's quiet there.'

'OK, Tom,' I said. I felt too ill to say no.

Tom took me by the arm and helped me walk back to my old house.

On the way he started talking.

'Steve told me about George,' said Tom.

'What did he say?'

'He said George took things from your flat: your watch, your CD player and your passport. He said the police want to talk to him.'

'The police don't *know* George took my things,' I said.

'You were stupid! You left me for him.'

'Tom, I don't want to talk about this.' I still felt ill.

We got to the door of my old house and Tom opened it.

'It's not too late,' he said. 'You can move back here.'

'No, Tom,' I said. 'I don't want to be with you any more.'

We went into the sitting room.

'I'll make coffee,' said Tom, 'while you think.'

He went into the kitchen.

I looked around. It was strange to be back in my old house. I walked over to the CDs and started looking at them.

'That's strange,' I thought. There was a little box behind the CDs. I picked it up and looked at it carefully. I opened the box. My gold watch! I looked at the back of the watch and saw N.R. – my initials.

I felt myself go cold.

Tom came in with the coffee. 'Well?' he said. 'What are you going to do now you know George took your things?'

'*George* took my things, Tom?' I asked.

'Yes.'

'So,' I said. My voice was hard. 'What's this, then?'

I showed him the watch. And Tom's face went white.

'Tom. Why is my watch here?'

He didn't speak.

'Did you go to my flat and take it?' I asked 'Did you take my other things, too?'

'Are you saying I steal things?' Tom asked.

'No, I know you don't need my things. So why *did* you take them?'

'Look, Nancy,' he said coldly. 'I gave you everything you wanted. But you left me for an asylum seeker with no money. I wanted to show you it was a mistake.'

'But it wasn't a mistake, Tom,' I said. 'George and I love each other.'

'He was using you to get a passport and money,' said Tom.

'No, he wasn't, Tom. George is a good kind man. He's kinder than you'll ever be!' I shouted. 'You wanted George out of my life. *That's* why you did this. And now the police want him.' I was so angry.

Tom tried once more.

'I'm not letting you go again,' he said. He was walking towards me.

I turned and opened the front door.

'Goodbye, Tom,' I said. I threw my watch at him and I ran out of the house.

I ran back to Harriet's house. 'Nancy!' she said, opening the door. 'What's wrong?'

'Harriet,' I said. 'Can I use your phone? I need the police.'

Chapter 15   *Our story*

The police found my passport, CD player and television in Tom's garage.

That night I stayed at Harriet's house.

In the morning, I tried to phone George again.

There was still no answer.

'Perhaps he isn't in the country any more,' I said to Harriet.

'What's his address?' she asked.

I found his letter in my bag and looked at the address at the top. 'Here,' I said, and I showed Harriet the letter.

'OK,' said Harriet, 'come on. We'll go there now. I'll drive.'

I put my arms around Harriet. She really was a good friend.

We got into Harriet's car. She drove fast.

'I can't believe Tom did this,' said Harriet. 'Where did he get a key from? Do you think he took it from our house when we were away?'

'I don't know,' I said. 'It isn't important. The police are talking to him now. He'll have to tell them everything.'

'Tom was so angry because you left him for an asylum seeker,' said Harriet, 'but I didn't think he could be so bad. I really didn't think he could do something like this.'

'I know,' I said. 'But when we were together, he was always angry with me. He thought he could stop me doing what I wanted. He stopped me writing. He didn't like me working. He always wanted to stop me doing things. Now he's trying to stop me seeing George.'

I felt terrible when I said George's name. I really wanted to see him again.

'I'm afraid,' I said to Harriet, as we stopped outside George's address. It was a big old house.

'What are you afraid of?' she asked.

'I'm afraid he isn't here. But I'm also afraid that he *is* here and he doesn't want to see me. Why hasn't he phoned me? Perhaps he doesn't want me anymore.'

I looked at Harriet.

'Go in and ask,' she said. 'You need to know.'

'Can you come with me?' I asked.

'No,' she replied. 'You need to go by yourself.'

I got out of the car and went in through the door of the building. There were some children playing inside by the stairs.

'Excuse me,' I said.

I saw in their eyes that they were afraid.

'Do you know a man called George?' I asked them.

They looked at each other, then smiled.

'George! George!' they sang. They started to laugh and ran up the stairs.

A few minutes later they came back again and ran out of the building into the street.

I looked at the empty stairs. Did they understand what I said? There was no one there.

I started to go out of the door.

'Nancy.'

I turned around.

George was standing at the top of the stairs.

'George,' I said.

He didn't move.

'George. Please speak to me. I need you.'

'Nancy,' he said quietly. 'I want you to know I didn't take your things from your flat.'

'George, I know you didn't,' I said.

'I went to your flat while you were away and I saw everything. Your television wasn't there, there was a broken glass. I thought, "People will think I did this." I was afraid, Nancy.'

'Is that why you went away from me?' I asked.

'Yes. When I saw your flat, I thought, "Nancy had a big home and lots of money before she met me. Now she lives in a small flat and people don't like her being with me". People don't understand. Perhaps we can't be together, Nancy.'

'George. Yes, I had a big house before I met you. But I wasn't happy.'

George began to walk down the stairs.

'But can I make you happy?' he asked.

'George!' I said. 'The last few days were the worst in my life. I thought about you all the time. I didn't know where you were or why you left me.'

'I thought about you, too,' he said.

He was next to me now.

I looked into his lovely brown eyes.

love you, George,' I said, 'and I want to be with you.'

I love you too, Nancy. But perhaps I'll have to leave. rhaps I'll have to go back to my country. We don't know t. Being together isn't going to be easy.'

46

'No. It isn't going to be easy, but we can help each other,' I said. 'Together, we can do anything.'

He smiled. Then he kissed me.

I knew then it was going to be all right. I knew George and I were going to be together.

George showed me that I could change. He showed me I could do anything I wanted. That's why I decided to write our story.

Cambridge English Readers

Look out for other titles in the series:

Level 2

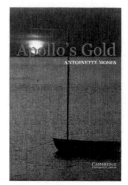

Different Worlds
Margaret Johnson

'In my world there are no birds singing. There are no noisy men working on the roads. No babies crying.'

Sam is like any other teenage girl except that is deaf. Now she is in love with Jim, but are their worlds too different?

Apollo's Gold
Antoinette Moses

Liz studies and teaches archaeology in Athens. She goes on holiday to the beautiful island of Sifnos. But when a mysterious yacht arrives, one of the local men dies, and Liz soon becomes involved with some very dangerous people.

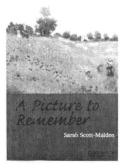

A Picture to Remember
Sarah Scott-Malden

Cristina Rinaldi works in Buenos Aires. One day she has an accident and can't remember some things. But there are two men who think she remembers too much, and they want to kill her before she tells the police what she saw.

Jojo's Story
Antoinette Moses

'There aren't any more days. There's just time. Time when it's dark and time when it's light. Everything is dead, so why not days too?'

Everyone in Jojo's village is dead, and ten-year-old Jojo is alone.